Declarations

of

Victory

by

Rhode Jean-Aleger

Published by:

McDougal & Associates
www.thepublishedword.com

McDougal & Associates is dedicated to the spreading of the Gospel of Jesus Christ to as many people as possible in the shortest time possible.

ISBN 978-1-940461-46-5

Printed on demand in the US, the UK and Australia
For Worldwide Distribution

Dedication

I will praise you with all my heart, glorify your name forever, LORD my God. Psalm 86:12, NAB

I dedicate this book to my God and Lord for the gift of writing He has bestowed upon me, which has enabled me to pen this book, *Declarations of Victory*.

I also dedicate this book to my loving husband, Vorbes Aleger, who has always stood by my side and supported me in all my endeavors. His unwavering love and encouragement have been my rock, and I am forever grateful for his presence in my life.

Acknowledgments

First and foremost, I want to express my gratitude to Victoria Kutch for her exceptional input and feedback. Her efforts have been invaluable, and I sincerely appreciate her hard work editing this work.

I am also grateful to Father Martin Ibeh, my mentor and brother in Christ, for his guidance and support in my spiritual journey. His wisdom and insight have been instrumental in shaping my writing and ministry.

My heartfelt thanks to my friends—Valentina Imhoff, Kathy Richards, Diane Hemsoth, Rose Alphee, Sherly Georges, Joann Kaczorowski, and Sr. Joann Gabbin—and my sister, Rhodeline Jean, for taking the time to read, review, and provide feedback on my work. Their invaluable contributions in refining my ideas have been greatly appreciated.

I also want to thank Mary Rousseau, my spiritual director, for walking with me in my spiritual journey and for her encouragement and support.

Finally, I offer my thanks and prayers to all my readers and the Jax Prayer Club and Marian Servant family. May God bless you abundantly and may the words in this book inspire all of you.

Endorsements

Declarations of Victory is a game-changer for anyone wishing to grow in their spiritual life. For years I have been looking for a simple resource to help myself and others change our mindsets and put on *"the mind of Christ"* (1 Corinthians 2:16) in every circumstance, and this is it. Thank you, Rhode, for your docility to the Holy Spirit and for creating this useful resource!

Valentina Imhoff
Founder of Fiat Career Coaching, LLC

Declarations of Victory is an inspiring book that declares God's promises over our life to help us live out our true identity in Christ. Anyone who embarks on this 31-day journey in faith can expect to unlock the promises of God's truth and gain strength for the journey. As you declare the truth, you will taste and see the goodness of the Lord!

Kathy Richards
Spiritual Director

Rhode is such an amazing woman of God. She hears His voice and obeys what He asks her to do. As a spiritual director, Rhode knows the power of God's words and the promise that comes with them. May everyone who reads *Declarations of Victory* be transformed forever as God's Word changes their mindset.

Diane Hemsoth
Spiritual Director
Member of Marian Servant of the Blessed Sacrament
Member of Friends of the Missions

God, who spoke everything into existence, created human beings in His image and likeness. When you have faith in the Lord, you can change your world through the words you speak. In this book, Rhode Aleger invites and encourages you to exercise your authority as a child of God and make positive declarations over whatever situations you face in life, so as to emerge victorious. *"You shall declare a thing and it will be established for you. So light will shine on your ways"* (Job 22:28).

Rev. L. C. Martin Ibeh
Diocese of St. Augustine
Author of Dawn at Last *&*
Flames Of Faith

I met Rhode Jean-Aleger in high school and have been close friends ever since. She is my sister from God. As they say, God places people in our lives for a reason. *"We know that all things work together for good for those who love God, who are called according to his purpose"* (Romans 8:28). She has been there for me in good and bad times, providing emotional, physical, and spiritual support. Rhode has helped me develop abilities I never thought I had and grow spiritually. She is an amazing servant of Christ who is always willing to assist and share God's love. Rhode boldly prophesied some of these declarations on my behalf based on the Word of God. Making these declarations and using these strategies has changed my life and helped me develop godly characteristics that now enable me to help others. I pray that everyone who uses these 31-day declarations will be blessed, healed, and equipped to overcome whatever storms cross their paths.

Rose Alphee, RN, MSN

Contents

BUT YOU ARE A CHOSEN PEOPLE, A ROYAL PRIESTHOOD, A HOLY NATION, GOD'S SPECIAL POSSESSION, THAT YOU MAY DECLARE THE PRAISES OF HIM WHO CALLED YOU OUT OF DARKNESS INTO HIS WONDERFUL LIGHT.

— 1 Peter 2:9, NIV

Introduction

*Let us hold fast to the confession of our hope without
wavering, for he who has promised is faithful.*
Hebrews 10:23, NRSV

God never ceases to amaze me! I am in awe of His
goodness and faithfulness! I was writing the second
chapter of a new book (not yet published) when the Lord
brought me to a complete STOP. Instead, He directed me
to write this thirty-one-day inspiration about our identity
and declarations in Christ. I sensed the Lord saying, "I
will help you, and you will return to your other writings
in no time." I was puzzled. I confided in two spiritual
friends who helped me regain my confidence. Simply,
this *Declarations of Victory* booklet is a blessing from the
Lord.

As I prayerfully wrote these declarations, I realized
there is hope for you and me–we who are broken,
wounded, and lost–if we can honestly pray for the grace
to change our mindset and accept the truth of who we
are in Christ, and to Whom we belong. A declaration in
Christ must move us to reject our own beliefs and ideol-
ogies and adapt to the things of God. We are victors in
and through Christ!

God's mind and thoughts are higher than ours. Until
we try to see things through the lens of God, we are not
living to the fullness of our potential. We are not yet
who He has called us to be. If we express a willingness

to see ourselves as He does and accept who we are in Him, He will help us experience the fullness of His truth. Through the knowledge of that truth, we can boldly come to His throne of grace and declare our heart's hopes and desires.

I hope and pray that in the next thirty-one days, through the pages of this book, God will instill in you His truth as you abide in His everlasting love. And that you, in turn, will deliberately live out your identity in Christ.

Rhode Jean-Aleger
Jacksonville, Florida

About the Layout

This *Declarations of Victory* booklet is divided into two parts. Part I consists of short reflections and statements of declaration in Jesus' name. Part II is a space for journaling.

Part I — Declarations in Christ!

The name of the LORD is a strong tower; the just run to it and are safe. Proverbs 18:10

In Jesus' name, we have access to power, authority, salvation, healing, protection, forgiveness, and redemption. By declaring the truth in the name of Jesus, we acknowledge our power in His name. His name carries the authority and power to transform us into His likeness and bring us better outcomes in every adverse situation.

Declarations in Christ are statements that describe who we are in Christ. These statements profess the truth about God's words and promises to us. The words we speak have power. As the Scriptures say, *"Death and life are in the power of the tongue; those who choose one shall eat its fruit"* (Proverbs 18:21). Therefore, we must pay attention to what we say, and speak only what is from God over our family, ourselves, and our situation. *"No foul language should come out of your mouths, but only such as is good for needed edification, that it may impart grace to those who hear"* (Ephesians 4:29). Hence, we should speak life, speak

God's blessing and promises, and watch God's miracles and wonders unfold in our lives and those of our family.

God's words are always valid, but when we declare them over our lives, we must align our hearts and ways of life with His commands, believe in His words and what He said about us, and abide in Him.

I hope these declarative statements will encourage you to stay grounded in Christ and recognize the Father's daily involvement in your life.

Part II — Journaling

Thus says the Lord, the God of Israel: Write in a book all the words that I have spoken to you.
Jeremiah 30:2, NRSV

Journaling is the art of recording our conversation with God in prayer, and journaling is very beneficial in the Christian life. Some benefits of journaling are:

- Creating a space for reflection, vulnerability, and sharing our joys and sadness with God.
- Recording any inspiration, feelings, and thoughts that arise in prayer.
- Strengthening our relationship with the Lord.
- Helping us to see our progress in spiritual life and discern God's will for us.
- Allowing us to heed God's words.
- Expressing our gratitude and joy, and praise God's goodness.

In scripture, we can see how David expressed himself in the Psalms. If he had not written his feelings down, we would not have these beautiful psalms today. Journaling helps us pass God's words on to the next generation.

We should revisit our journal entries regularly to refresh our memory of God's inspirations and promises. These memories can motivate and encourage us in difficult times. I encourage all of you to have a spiritual journal and to review it from time to time.

I have provided some space in the book so you can prayerfully write your declaration in your own words. I hope you let God's hand be the pen that writes every word in these journal sections.

PRAYER: *Lord Jesus, thank You for Your words and the inspiration received through journaling. Lord, allow us to see Your handwriting in our lives. It is Your name we pray. Amen!*

A Prayer of Victory!

Do not conform yourselves to this age but be transformed by the renewal of your mind, that you may discern what is the will of God, what is good and pleasing and perfect.

Romans 12:2

Before we begin praying about the declarations in Christ, let us pray for the Lord to deliver us from any ungodly mindsets. I invite you to reflect on this prayer and let Jesus' words bring deliverance and healing to your heart.

- Lord Jesus, deliver me from the concept of "it is about me, myself, and I."
- Deliver me from self-addiction.
- Deliver me from self-centered attitudes and selfishness.
- Deliver me from the mindset that I am better than others.
- Deliver me from self-reliance.
- Deliver me from the attitude that my opinions are more valuable.
- Deliver me from self-righteousness.
- Deliver me from the belief that I am worthless.
- Deliver me from the spirit of jealousy of others.
- Deliver me from the spirit of competition.

- Deliver me from being judgmental.
- Deliver me from my unwillingness to see others' points of view.
- Deliver me from the fear of making a mistake.
- Deliver me from the fear of taking risks and acting boldly for Your glory.
- Lord, give me the will to change my unholy mindsets and ways.[1]

In Jesus' name, I declare that I have been healed and redeemed from my ungodly mindsets, and in Jesus' name, I now declare this scripture for the renewal of my mind:

Finally, brothers, whatever is true, whatever is honorable, whatever is just, whatever is pure, whatever is lovely, whatever is gracious, if there is any excellence and if there is anything worthy of praise, think about these things. Keep on doing what you have learned and received and heard and seen in me. Then the God of peace will be with you.   Philippians 4:8-9

PRAYER: *Lord Jesus, thank You for Your deliverance and the healing of my mind. In Your name I pray. Amen!*

---

1. This prayer is inspired by the Litany Trust.

JOURNAL: WRITE HERE YOUR OWN PRAYER
OF DELIVERANCE AND VICTORY

Day 2

A Statement of Declaration About Our Prayer Life!

In the same way, the Spirit too comes to the aid of our weakness; for we do not know how to pray as we ought, but the Spirit itself intercedes with inexpressible groanings. Romans 8:26

Prayer is an intimate and honest conversation with the Lord about our heart's desires, concerns, and His will for us. We must rely on the Holy Spirit to pray for us and with us. He will give us the right inspirations in prayer. I declare in Jesus' name:

- I will devote my life to prayer by starting and ending my day with prayer and be thankful in all things (see Colossians 4:2).
- I will approach my Lord with reverence but not with fear and uncertainty (see Hebrews 4:16).
- I will not be afraid to come to the Lord as I am and with all that I have (see Matthew 11:27-30).
- I will be resilient in prayer and meditate on God's words (see Ephesians 6:18).

PRAYER: *Thank You, Lord Jesus, for the powerful gift of prayer. In Your name I pray. Amen!*

JOURNAL — WRITE HERE YOUR OWN DECLARATIONS AND/OR PRAYER ABOUT YOUR PRAYER LIFE

A Statement of Declaration About Our Identity in Christ!

But to those who did accept him he gave power to become children of God, to those who believe in his name, who were born not by natural generation nor by human choice nor by a man's decision but of God.   John 1:12-13

Knowing who we are in Christ helps us accept the truth about ourselves and reject the enemy's lies about our identity. I declare in Jesus' name:

- God knew me and set me apart before I was born (see Jeremiah 1:5).
- I am a daughter/son of God (see Galatians 4:7).
- I am the clay in God's hands (see Jeremiah 18:6)
- I am guarded as the apple of God's eyes (see Psalm 17:8)

PRAYER: *Thank You, Lord, for being a good Father. In Your name I pray. Amen!*

JOURNAL: WRITE HERE YOUR OWN DECLARATION AND/OR PRAYER ABOUT YOUR IDENTITY

Day 4

A Statement of Declaration Against Anxiety and Worries!

Blessed are those who trust in the LORD; the LORD will be their trust. They are like a tree planted beside the waters that stretches out its roots to the stream.

Jeremiah 17:7

Keeping our minds and spirits fixed on Christ helps us receive His peace in all circumstances. Therefore, keep your minds on things above, not on earthly things (see Colossians 3:3). Let us continue to bear fruit in all seasons of life. I declare in Jesus' name:

- I am not anxious or worried about anything but will come to Him with every petition and request (see Philippians 4:6-7).
- I am not worried about my life. God, my Father, knows what I need (see Matthew 6:25-34).
- I have no fear over those who kill the body because they cannot kill my soul (see Matthew 10:26-31)
- I cast my anxieties on the Lord because He cares for me (see 1 Peter 5: 7).
- I will continue to bear fruit regardless of my circumstances (see John 15:16).

PRAYER: *Thank You, Lord Jesus, for Your supernatural peace. In Your name I pray. Amen!*

JOURNAL: WRITE HERE YOUR OWN DECLARATION AND/OR PRAYER AGAINST ANXIETY AND WORRIES

Day 5

A Statement of Declaration Against Fear!

Do not fear: I am with you; do not be anxious: I am your God. I will strengthen you, I will help you, I will uphold you with my victorious right hand. Isaiah 41:10

Fear can paralyze us and stop us from experiencing the fullness of God and His promises. Therefore, let us pray for the grace to trust in the Lord with all our hearts. I declare in Jesus' name:

- I am not a slave to fear and will not live in fear because I am a child of God (see Romans 8:15-17).
- I fear no evil because God is with me. His rod and staff comfort me (see Psalm 23:4).
- I fear no evil near my tent because God will command His angels to guard me (see Psalm 91:9-11).
- I fear no evil, for God will uphold me with His victorious right hand (see Isaiah 41:10)

PRAYER: *Thank You, Lord Jesus, for I am no longer a slave to fear, and I am walking in the freedom that You have given me. In Your name I pray. Amen!*

26

JOURNAL: WRITE HERE YOUR OWN DECLARATION AND/OR PRAYER AGAINST FEAR

Day 6

A Statement of Declaration Against Discouragement!

Therefore, my beloved brothers, be firm, steadfast, always fully devoted to the work of the Lord, knowing that in the Lord your labor is not in vain.   1 Corinthians 15:58

Discouragement prevents us from focusing on God's plan and purpose for us. Instead of surrendering everything to the Lord, it chains us to our problems. I declare in Jesus' name:

- I am never alone; the Lord goes before and after me. He will never forsake me (see Deuteronomy 31:8).
- I will cast all my burdens on my Lord, who will sustain me (see Psalm 55:22).
- I am strong because I hope in the Lord (see Psalm 31:24)
- God is with me; who can be against me (see Romans 8:31)

PRAYER: *Thank You, Lord Jesus, for the spirit of courage. In Your name I pray. Amen!*

JOURNAL: WRITE HERE YOUR OWN DECLARATION AND/OR PRAYER AGAINST DISCOURAGEMENT

Day 7

A Statement of Declaration Against Doubt!

But he should ask in faith, not doubting, for the one who doubts is like a wave of the sea that is driven and tossed about by the wind. For that person must not suppose that he will receive anything from the Lord, since he is a man of two minds, unstable in all his ways. James 1:6-8

Doubt can cause worries and uncertainties. It prevents us from living meaningfully in Christ. Even when we are confused about life and see no light at the end of the tunnel, God is always with us. For instance, some of us doubt the mercy and forgiveness of God and God's presence in our circumstances. I declare in Jesus' name:

- I will not lean on my understanding but trust the Lord (see Proverbs 3:5-6).
- I will not worry about tomorrow, for God holds my tomorrow (see Matthew 6:34).
- I will trust in God, for nothing is impossible with Him (see Luke 1:37).
- I will hold to my Lord for wisdom and understanding (see James 1:5-8).

PRAYER: *Thank You, Lord Jesus, for the grace to keep our minds fixed on You. In Your name I pray. Amen!*

JOURNAL: WRITE HERE YOUR OWN DECLARATION AND/OR PRAYER AGAINST DOUBT

Day 8

A Statement of Declaration Against Pride!

For by the grace given to me I tell everyone among you not to think of himself more highly than one ought to think, but to think soberly, each according to the measure of faith that God has apportioned.   Romans 12:3

Pride is the root of all evil. It is a poison for the soul. We must renounce pride daily and pray for a spirit of humility to live in us. If we ask, the Holy Spirit will help us. I declare in Jesus' name:

- I reject the spirit of pride and accept the spirit of humility (see James 4:10).
- I will overcome the spirit of pride with God's grace. I can do all things in and through Christ (see Philippians 4:13)
- I receive the spirit of fear of the Lord and prayerfully fight to avoid a prideful heart (see Proverbs 8:13).
- God will increase in my life, and I will decrease (see John 3:30).

PRAYER: *Thank You, Lord Jesus, for the spirit of humility. In Your name I pray. Amen!*

JOURNAL: WRITE HERE YOUR OWN DECLARATION AND/OR PRAYER AGAINST PRIDE

Day 9

A Statement of Declaration Against Financial Burdens!

In every way I have shown you that by hard work of that sort we must help the weak, and keep in mind the words of the Lord Jesus who himself said, "It is more blessed to give than to receive."　　　　　　Acts 20:35

In times of financial burdens, fix your eyes on our heavenly Father, who is rich in kindness and mercy. He cannot be outdone in generosity. Pray! Pray, do not lose sight of God in these difficult times. I declare in Jesus' name:

- I will help those in need (see Galatians 6:2).
- I will ask and receive; I will search and find; I will knock, and the door will be opened for me (see Matthew 7:7).
- My God will supply my every need according to His riches (see Philippians 4:19).
- My God will send help from above and will support me (see Psalm 20:2)
- My God will satisfy my heart's desire (see Psalm 20:4).

PRAYER: *Thank You, Lord Jesus, for Your daily bread. In Your name I pray. Amen!*

JOURNAL: WRITE HERE YOUR OWN DECLARATION AND/OR PRAYER AGAINST FINANCIAL BURDENS

Day 10

A Statement of Declaration Against Despair!

Are not two sparrows sold for a small coin? Yet not one of them falls to the ground without your Father's knowledge. Even all the hairs of your head are counted. So do not be afraid; you are worth more than many sparrows.
Matthew 10:29-31

It's easy to lose hope during the trials of life. Let us ask the Lord for the grace to hope and pray even when we do not see a light at the end of the tunnel. Let us depend more on the Lord and surrender our plans and lives to Him. I declare in Jesus' name:

- I may be afflicted, but I am not crushed nor perplexed, and I will not be driven to despair (see 2 Corinthians 4:8)
- I am confident that God will rescue me, and I set my hope on Him (see 2 Corinthians 1:10-11).
- I will not be afraid; I am confident that I will see the goodness of the Lord, for He is my light, my salvation, and the stronghold of my life (see Psalm 27:1-2).
- I will wait for the Lord, my soul will wait, and I will hope in His words (see Psalm 130:5)

PRAYER: *Thank You, Lord Jesus, for the hope I have in You. In Your name I pray. Amen!*

JOURNAL: WRITE HERE YOUR OWN DECLARATION AND/OR PRAYER AGAINST DESPAIR

Statement of Declaration Against Addictions!

"Everything is lawful for me," but not everything is beneficial. "Everything is lawful for me," but I will not let myself be dominated by anything.

1 Corinthians 6:12

Many think people are only addicted to food or illicit substances like alcohol. However, we can be addicted to self, certain sins, shopping, work, TV, social media, etc. We must pay attention to the actions in our lives that do not bring glory to God. I declare in Jesus' name:

- I will not be mastered by anything of this world but by God alone (see 1 Corinthians 6:12)
- I will say "no" to ungodliness and worldly passions and "yes" to a life of self-control, uprightness, and godliness (see Titus 2:12).
- I will glorify God in my body (see 1 Corinthian 6:20).
- The Lord delivers me from temptations and will not let me fall into sin (see Matthew 6:13)

PRAYER: *Thank You, Lord Jesus, for the spirit of self-control. In Your name I pray. Amen!*

JOURNAL: WRITE HERE YOUR OWN DECLARATION AND/OR PRAYER AGAINST ADDICTION

Day 12

A Statement of Declaration of Forgiveness!

In him we have redemption by his blood, the forgiveness of transgressions, in accord with the riches of his grace.
Ephesians 1:7

God's forgiveness is a gift. When we genuinely repent, God's forgiveness cleans, heals and redeems us from our past sins and makes us whole again. I declare in Jesus' name:

- I admit my sins and confess them, and God forgives me for my wrongdoing (see 1 John 1:9).
- I forgive myself for trusting man more than God (see Psalm 118:8-9).
- I forgive those who have hurt me in all areas of life (see Ephesians 4:32, Matthew 6:14)
- I forgive those who have taken me for granted. I expect nothing from them in return (see Luke 6:35).
- I let go of all my grudges with God's grace (see Ephesians 4:31-32)

PRAYER: *Thank You, Lord Jesus, for forgiving and loving me. In Your name I pray. Amen!*

JOURNAL: WRITE HERE YOUR OWN DECLARATION AND/OR PRAYER OF FORGIVENESS

Day 13

A Statement of Declaration About Healing!

Heal me, LORD, that I may be healed; save me, that I may be saved, for you are my praise. Jeremiah 17:14

Let us not allow our physical illness or discomfort to prevent us from accomplishing God's mission. Let us implore the Lord for the gift of healing. I declare in Jesus' name:

- God is healing all my ailments, for God is my Healer (see Exodus 15:26).
- God is healing my broken heart and is binding up my wounds (see Psalm 147:3)
- God is healing me from spiritual blindness. He will pour fresh water over me, and I shall be cleansed (see Ezekiel 36:25).
- God has answered my request, and I praise and thank Him (see Psalms 28:6-7).

PRAYER: *Thank You, Lord Jesus, for Your healing and deliverance. In Your name I pray. Amen!*

JOURNAL: WRITE HERE YOUR OWN DECLARATION AND/OR PRAYER ABOUT HEALING

Day 14

A Statement of Declaration of God's Mercy!

Praise the LORD, for he is good; for his mercy endures forever.   Psalm 136:1

God is rich in mercy because of His great love for us; even when we are dead in our transgressions, He brings us to life (see Ephesians 2: 4-7). God's mercy and love cost Jesus His life. We must pray that we all accept His mercy and love. God's ocean of mercy is greater than our sins. I declare in Jesus' name:

- I receive and accept God's mercy, which is new every morning (see Lamentations 3:22-23).
- I am healed of my sins and diseases (see Psalm 103:3).
- I am redeemed by the precious blood of Christ (see Ephesians 1:7).
- I pray for the grace to be merciful to others as Jesus commanded me (see Matthew 5:7).

PRAYER: *Thank You, Lord Jesus, for Your goodness and mercy. In Your name I pray. Amen!*

JOURNAL: WRITE HERE YOUR OWN DECLARATION AND/OR PRAYER ABOUT HEALING

Day 15

A Statement of Declaration About God's Favor!

May the favor of the LORD our God be ours. Prosper the work of our hands! Prosper the work of our hands!

Psalm 90:17

We don't deserve God's favor, but He blesses us out of His love. Therefore, let us humbly receive God's favor and share it with others. I declare in Jesus' name:

- I am seated with God in heavenly places and highly favored (see Ephesians 2:6).
- I have received authority and power in Jesus' name (see Matthew 28:18-20).
- I have received all spiritual gifts and blessings in the heavens (see Ephesians 1:3).
- I have received grace upon grace out of God's fullness (see John 1:16).

PRAYER: *Thank You, Lord Jesus, for Your favor and grace. In Your name I pray. Amen!*

JOURNAL: WRITE HERE YOUR OWN DECLARATION AND/OR PRAYER ABOUT GOD'S FAVOR

Day 16

A Statement of Declaration About God's Blessing!

Moreover, God is able to make every grace abundant for you, so that in all things, always having all you need, you may have an abundance for every good work.

2 Corinthian 9:8

When we think of God's blessing, we ought to witness to all and confess that Jesus Christ is Lord for the glory of God. Let us remain grateful in all circumstances. I declare in Jesus' name:

- I am blessed beyond measure (see Numbers 6:24-26, Ephesians 1:3).
- My family is blessed (see Numbers 6:24-26).
- I am blessed to be a blessing (see Genesis 12:1-3).
- Everything around and about me is blessed because God is with me always, and He has equipped me for every good work (see 2 Corinthians 9:8).

PRAYER: *Thank You, Lord Jesus, for the many blessings You have bestowed upon me. In Your name I pray. Amen!*

JOURNAL: WRITE HERE YOUR OWN DECLARATION AND/OR PRAYER ABOUT GOD'S BLESSING

Day 17

A Statement of Declaration About My Relationship with Others!

Above all, let your love for one another be intense, because love covers a multitude of sins.   1 Peter 4:8

Living life alone lacks purpose. Life is more meaningful when we travel with others who are always there for us. *"How very good and pleasant it is when kindred live together in unity!"* **(Psalm 133:1, NRSV). I declare in Jesus' name:**

- All my relationships (family/friends/colleagues) will be pure, pleasant, stable, and peaceful (see Psalm 133).
- I will care for those whom God has entrusted to me (see Deuteronomy 15:7-11).
- I will nurture all with love and prayers (see 1 Corinthian 16:14).
- I am willing to accept the sacrifices that love demands (see Proverb 17:17).

PRAYER: *Thank You, Lord Jesus, for the people You have put in my life. Help me be a blessing to them today and forever. In Your name I pray. Amen!*

JOURNAL: WRITE HERE YOUR OWN DECLARATION AND/ OR PRAYER ABOUT YOUR RELATIONSHIP WITH OTHERS

Day 18

A Statement of Declaration About Our Authority in Christ!

The Spirit of the Lord God is upon me, because the Lord has anointed me; he has sent me to bring good news to the afflicted, to bind up the brokenhearted, to proclaim liberty to the captives, release to the prisoners, to announce a year of favor from the Lord and a day of vindication by our God; to comfort all who mourn; to place on those who mourn in Zion a diadem instead of ashes, to give them oil of gladness instead of mourning, a glorious mantle instead of a faint spirit. Isaiah 61:1-3

We all have the authority to continue Jesus' mission on earth. Let us not look to our brothers and sisters to continue Jesus' work. Let us implore Him to remove any self-centered spirit from us so that we are compassionate and open to the needs of others. I declare in Jesus' name:

- I have the authority to lay hands on the sick, and they will recover (see Isaiah 61:1).
- I have the authority to help the captives receive freedom in Christ (see Isaiah 61:1).
- I accept the obligation to feed the hungry and the poor (see Matthew 25:31-40)

PRAYER: *Thank You, Lord Jesus, for giving me authority in Your mighty name. In Your name I pray. Amen!*

JOURNAL: WRITE HERE YOUR DECLARATION AND/OR PRAYER ABOUT YOUR AUTHORITY IN CHRIST

Day 19

A Statement of Declaration Over Our Purpose!

But you are "a chosen race, a royal priesthood, a holy nation, a people of his own, so that you may announce the praises" of him who called you out of darkness into his wonderful light. 1 Peter 2:9

We were not created to merely exist; we were created for good works and to fulfill God's purpose for His greater glory. I declare in Jesus' name:

- I will accomplish the work for which God has prepared me (see Ephesians 2:10)
- I am a holy nation, a royal priesthood, dedicated to God's service (see 1 Peter 2:9)
- I am called out of darkness into God's marvelous light (see 1 Peter 2:9).
- The Lord's purpose will prevail in me (see Proverb 19:21)
- God's plan and purpose for me will stand firm forever (see Psalm 33:11)

PRAYER: *Thank You, Lord Jesus, for defining Your plans and purpose for me. In Your name I pray. Amen!*

JOURNAL: WRITE HERE YOUR OWN DECLARATION AND/OR PRAYER ABOUT YOUR PURPOSE

Day 20

A Statement of Declaration About My Life's Mission!

He [Jesus] said to them, "Go into the whole world and pro-claim the gospel to every creature." Mark 16:15

We must pray to be obedient to the inspirations of the Holy Spirit while making every effort to respond to God's assignment with an open heart. If He calls us, He will equip us to do His work. I declare in Jesus' name:

- My God partners with me in His work of ministry. He is my guiding light (see Psalm 27:1-2).
- I will not put God in a box. I will dream big and depend on Him for everything (see Psalm 37:4-5).
- I will arise and shine in God's work, for I am His daughter/son (see Isaiah 60:1-2).
- I will step out of my comfort zone to do God's will and work. God has a plan for me. I will not be fear-ful or doubtful (see Jeremiah 29:11, 2 Timothy 1:7).
- I will permit my Lord to transform me to do His work. I am His vessel (see Romans 12:1-2).
- I will make God known through my words and deeds (see Colossians 3:17).

PRAYER: *Thank You, Lord Jesus, for Your mantle of protection. In Your name I pray. Amen!*

JOURNAL: WRITE HERE YOUR OWN DECLARATION AND/OR PRAYER ABOUT YOUR LIFE'S MISSION

Day 21

A Statement of Declaration Against Life's Battles!

You will not have to fight in this encounter. Take your places, stand firm, and see the salvation of the LORD; he will be with you, Judah and Jerusalem. Do not fear or be dismayed.　　　　　　　2 Chronicles 20:17

No one can fight the power of God; that is why I am confident that with Jesus, my Refuge and Fortress, I will be victorious in every battle. Therefore, I will not be disheartened. I declare in Jesus' name:

- No weapon formed against me will prosper (see Isaiah 54:17).
- The enemy means evil against me; God means it for good (see Genesis 50:20).
- I will be successful in using the armor of God to fight my every battle (see Ephesians 6:10-17).
- The Lord will fight all my battles for me, and I will remain silent (see Exodus 14:14).

PRAYER: *Thank You, Lord Jesus, for Your mantle of protection. In Your name I pray. Amen!*

JOURNAL: WRITE HERE YOUR OWN DECLARATION AND/OR PRAYER AGAINST LIFE'S BATTLES

Day 22

A Statement of Declaration of Victory in Our Spiritual Life!

Call on Me in the day of trouble; I will deliver you, and you shall glorify Me.   Psalm 50:15, NRSV

We battle with unwanted sins, vices, and lies of the enemy. However, every time we make spiritual progress, get rid of sins, and reject lies, we are victorious in the Lord. I declare in Jesus' name:

- I reject the lies of the enemy and accept God, who is the Way and the Truth (see John 8:44).
- I will overcome vices, sins, and temptations with the assistance of the Holy Spirit (see Galatians 5:16-26).
- I will increase in virtue and gifts of the Holy Spirit through prayer and fasting (see 2 Peter 1:5).
- My life will be a living testimony. I am victorious in the Lord (see 1 Corinthians 15:57).

PRAYER: *Thank You, Lord Jesus, for Your victory in my life. In Your name I pray. Amen!*

JOURNAL: WRITE HERE YOUR OWN DECLARATION AND/OR PRAYER OF VICTORY

A Statement of Declaration of Hope!

Therefore, we are not discouraged; rather, although our outer self is wasting away, our inner self is being renewed day by day. 2 Corinthians 4:16

In times of uncertainty, fix your eyes firmly on the Lord to renew your spirit and gain the strength to overcome any challenge. I declare in Jesus' name:

- I will rejoice in hope, be patient in tribulation, and constant in prayer (see Romans 12:12).
- I will hope in the Lord despite the chaos of life (see Psalm 130:7).
- My God, the Supplier of hope will fill me with all joy and peace as I trust in Him (see Romans 15:13).
- I will overflow with hope by the power of the Holy Spirit (see Romans 15:13).

PRAYER: *Thank You, Lord Jesus, for You are the virtue of hope. In Your name I pray. Amen!*

JOURNAL: WRITE HERE YOUR OWN DECLARATION AND/OR PRAYER OF HOPE

Day 24

A Statement of Declaration of Faith!

Let us hold unwaveringly to our confession that gives us hope, for he who made the promise is trustworthy.
Hebrews 10:23

The declaration of our faith describes our identity in Christ and the hallmark of our spiritual life. I declare in Jesus' name:

- I believe in God the Father's mercy and love for me (see 1 John 3:1).
- I believe Jesus Christ died out of His love for me (see John 3:16).
- I permit the Lord to baptize me with the Holy Spirit and fire and to set me on fire for the Lord (see Matthew 3:11).
- I will walk by faith and not by sight (see 2 Corinthians 5:7)
- My faith is being renewed, is unshakable, and will move mountains (see Matthew 17:20).

PRAYER: *Thank You, Lord Jesus, for the virtue of faith. In Your name I pray. Amen!*

JOURNAL: WRITE HERE YOUR OWN
DECLARATION AND/OR PRAYER OF FAITH

Day 25

A Statement of Declaration of God's Love!

As the Father loves me, so I also love you. Remain in my love. If you keep my commandments, you will remain in my love, just as I have kept my Father's commandments and remain in his love. John 15:9-10

Many of us know God's love from the Bible or spiritual readings, but how about letting the knowledge of His love take root in our hearts and minds? I declare in Jesus' name:

- God's love is free; I do not have to perform to receive it (see John 3:16).
- I depend on God in all things. My hope is in Him (see Psalm 62:6-9).
- God loved me first, so I love in return (see 1 John 4:19)
- God cannot deny me because He is faithful to me (see 2 Timothy 2:13).
- God's love is enough for me (see Ephesians 1:23).

PRAYER: *Thank You, Lord Jesus, for Your unmeasurable love. In Your name I pray. Amen!*

JOURNAL: WRITE HERE YOUR OWN DECLARATION AND/OR PRAYER ABOUT GOD'S LOVE

Day 26

A Statement of Declaration About Humility!

Have among yourselves the same attitude that is also yours in Christ Jesus, who, though he was in the form of God, did not regard equality with God something to be grasped. Rather, he emptied himself, taking the form of a slave, coming in human likeness; and found human in appearance, he humbled himself, becoming obedient to death, even death on a cross. Philippians 2:5-8

Jesus was both man and God, yet He was obedient to His Father and accepted His holy will. We must make deliberate efforts to cultivate the virtue of humility. Please help me, God. I declare in Jesus' name:

- I will humble myself before my Lord (see James 4:10)
- I will think of myself last (see Matthew 20:16).
- I will serve with the heart of Jesus and not expect to be served (see Matthew 10:43-45).

PRAYER: *Thank You, Lord Jesus, for teaching me the virtue of humility. In Your name I pray. Amen!*

JOURNAL: WRITE HERE YOUR OWN DECLARATION AND/OR PRAYER ABOUT HUMILITY

Day 27

A Statement of Declaration About Peace!

Strive for peace with everyone, and for that holiness without which no one will see the Lord.

Hebrews 12:14

There is war in the world because we have no peace within us. We must seek and pursue peace (see Psalm 34:14). Therefore, let us pray for peace with God and peace in our hearts, families, and communities in order to increase peace in the world. I declare in Jesus' name:

- I have the peace of Jesus (see John 14:27)
- Nothing will disturb me because I carry the mark of Jesus within me (see Galatians 6:17)
- I rest assured that God controls my life (see Jeremiah 10:23).
- I will choose peace today and forever (see Hebrews 12:14).
- The Holy Spirit does not live in chaos, so neither do I, because I am His temple (see 1 Corinthian 6:19).

PRAYER: *Thank You, Lord Jesus, for Your peace that is beyond understanding. In Your name I pray. Amen!*

JOURNAL: WRITE HERE YOUR OWN DECLARATION AND/OR PRAYER ABOUT PEACE

Day 28

My Positive Declarations!

In Christ you have been brought to fullness. He is the head over every power and authority. Colossians 2:10, NIV

Words matter! Let us reject negativity, start fresh, and boldly declare in Jesus' name:

- I am complete in the Lord, and I lack nothing (see Psalm 23:)
- I am not my mistakes, guilt, or shame, but I am the apple of God's eye (see Psalm 17:8)
- I am God's beloved, and no one can take that away from me (see Ephesians 1:6).
- I am fruitful in all things by God's grace (see Genesis 1:28).
- I can do all things through Christ who gives me strength (see Philippians 4:13).
- I dedicate my life to the Lord in everything .
- I will accomplish my set goals for this year (name them).
- I stand tall, dream big, aspire to great things and works, and I am the best version of myself—no matter the circumstances (see Ephesians 2:10).

72

- The blessings are pouring down on me, and I praise the Lord without reservation from morning to night (see Malachi 3:10).

Have you recently asked God to bless you or declared His promises upon your life? When we implore God to make positive changes, we can speak miracles into our lives. We must not allow negative thoughts to take root in our hearts and minds. Whenever we sense a thought that is not from God, we must reject and renounce it immediately through prayer. As we change our thought processes to align with God, He pours His favor upon us, and the direction of our lives will also shift positively.

If things are not going as expected, let us cry out to God and seek His blessings and favor, just as Jacob did when he wrestled with the angel: *"I will not let you go until you bless me"* (Genesis 32:27, NAB). Let us never stop seeking God's blessing and favor, for His favor can change everything.

PRAYER: *Lord Jesus, I need more of You. Fill me with more of Your Spirit, grace, love, and mercy. In Your name I pray. Amen!*

JOURNAL: WRITE HERE YOUR OWN DECLARATIONS IN CHRIST

_____

_____

_____

_____

_____

_____

_____

_____

_____

_____

_____

_____

_____

_____

_____

_____

_____

_____

_____

_____

_____

_____

_____

_____

_____

_____

_____

_____

Day 29

A declaration of Overflowing Blessings!

I will give you hidden treasures, riches stored in secret places, so that you may know that I am the LORD, the God of Israel, who summons you by name.

Isaiah 45:3, NIV

God is the God of the impossible. He wants to bless us more than we can ever imagine or expect. Open your hearts, minds, and souls to receive the Father's blessing. As children of God, let us "announce a year of favor from the Lord and a day of vindication by our God" (Isaiah 61:2, NABRE). In Jesus' name, I declare that our God will bless us with the following:

- An increase in our spiritual gifts and talents
- An increase in spiritual blessings beyond our imagination
- Courage over discouragement
- Faith over fear
- Health over sickness
- Hope over despair
- Joy over sadness
- Love over hatred
- Peace over chaos

- Power over helplessness
- Prosperity over poverty
- Success over failure
- Strength over weakness
- Victory over defeat

Although God is always willing to bless us, we must also do our part. For instance, if we pray for the Lord to bless us with peace, we must actively pursue peace by creating peace in our environment. The Scriptures tell us: *"Strive for peace with everyone, and for that holiness without which no one will see the Lord* (Hebrew 12:14, NAB). Similarly, if we desire to experience more love in our lives, we must be willing to make sacrifices and prioritize others. *"Put on then, as God's chosen ones, holy and beloved, heartfelt compassion, kindness, humility, gentleness, and patience, bearing with one another and forgiving one another"* (Colossians 3:12-13 NAB). It is up to us to take the first step, and God will do the rest. Therefore, let us work hand in hand with God to receive His overflowing blessings.

PRAYER: *Lord Jesus, thank You for blessing me beyond my imagination. In Your name I pray. Amen!*

JOURNAL: WRITE HERE YOUR OWN DECLARATION AND/ OR PRAYER ABOUT YOUR OVERFLOWING BLESSING

A Declaration of Praise from Psalm 150!

Through him [then] let us continually offer God a sacrifice of praise, that is, the fruit of lips that confess his name.   Hebrews 13:15, NAB

Praising and worshiping the Lord are prayers that break down walls, heal our wounds, and bring us closer to Him. They renew and transform our hearts and minds and give us strength to face life's challenges. When we praise God, we experience His grace and mercy.

In his *Manual for Spiritual Warfare*,[2] Paul Thigpen tells us, "Worship is a spiritual weapon. When we worship God, we enter into His presence in a powerful way. Because demons tremble at His presence, they are reluctant to follow us there." Therefore, let us take time to lift our voices and praise the One who truly deserves it all!

- Hallelujah!
- I praise God in His holy sanctuary.
- I praise Him in the mighty dome of Heaven.
- I praise Him for His mighty deeds,
- I praise Him for His great majesty.
- I praise Him with blasts upon the horn,

---

2. *Manual for Spiritual Warfare*, Paul Thigpen, pg. 39, 2014

- I praise Him with harp and lyre.
- I praise Him with tambourines and dance,
- I praise Him with strings and pipes.
- I praise Him with crashing cymbals,
- I praise Him with sounding cymbals.
- Let every breath I take give praise to the LORD.
- Let everything around me give praise to the LORD.
- I give praise to the LORD today and forever!
- Hallelujah!

When I struggle to find the right words to praise and worship God, I often turn to the book of Psalms. As I personalize the Psalm, I allow the Holy Spirit to guide me in expressing words of adoration to God. I invite you to pray with the Psalms and declare the goodness of God through them.

PRAYER: *Lord Jesus, give me the grace to praise You without ceasing. In Your name I pray. Amen!*

JOURNAL: WRITE HERE YOUR OWN DECLARATION OF PRAISE TO THE LORD

Day 31

Arise and Shine!

*Arise! Shine, for your light has come, the glory of the
LORD has dawned upon you. Though darkness covers the
earth, and thick clouds, the people. Upon you the Lord
will dawn, and over you his glory will be seen. Nations
shall walk by your light, kings by the radiance of your
dawning.* Isaiah 60:1-3, NAB

God wants to rescue us from the power of darkness
and bring us to the fullness of His light. Put away your
cowardliness, fear, shyness, and timidity. God is calling
you to be bold in the faith, to *"arise and shine"* in His light
and glory:

- At your job/work
- With your family
- In your churches and ministries
- In all new endeavors
- As an ambassador for Christ
- As a leader in your community
- Wherever you are on this Earth

We were created for greatness and to continue the
work of Jesus. He said in John 12:12-13 (NIV), *"Very truly*

I tell you, whoever believes in me will do the works I have been doing, and they will do even greater things than these, because I am going to the Father. And I will do whatever you ask in my name, so that the Father may be glorified in the Son." We are not limited in any way, but we were born with inspiration, creativity, knowledge, imagination, and understanding from the Holy Spirit.

"Arise and shine" moments may include praying for or with a stranger or family member, testifying to what God has done for you, serving the poor and those in need, and more. Do not be afraid to *"arise and shine"* because you are a light to all those whom you encounter. When we partner with God, our sphere of influence will increase, and we can make a greater impact for Him, touching more lives.

Let us pray that God will give us the grace to see and seize every opportunity to serve Him without reservation. Let us also pray that God will bless us with the strength to use our spiritual gifts, blessings, and talents. We need to understand that we may have to make some personal sacrifices to touch lives in this world, but I promise you, it is well worth it.

When you say yes to God, *"arise and shine"* moments will show up supernaturally, and God will give you the right tools to operate. Say "Yes" to God today. "Arise and shine!" Be great! Be innovative! Go make a difference in the world around you!

PRAYER: *Lord Jesus, give me clarity so I know how to shine Your light in all I do and whenever I go. I thank You and praise You with all my heart. In Your name I pray. Amen!*

JOURNAL: WRITE HERE YOUR OWN DECLARATION AND/OR PRAYER ABOUT YOUR "ARISE AND SHINE" MOMENTS

Author Contact Page

You may contact Rhode Jean-Aleger directly in the following ways:

Email: Jaxprayerclub@gmail.com

Website: www.Jaxprayerclub.com

From HIM and through HIM and to HIM!

Inspiration for Every Day of the Year

Rhode Jean-Aleger

ISBN: 978-1-950398-75-1, 5 X 8, 388 pages